# BASIC
# MAT CUTTING

*Basic Mat Cutting*
by Vivian Kistler, CPF, GCF

Columba Publishing Company, Akron, Ohio
© 2001, 1998, 1996, 1995  Logan Graphic
Products, Inc., Wauconda, Illinois
Second Edition
Printed in the United States of America

30  29  28  27  26  25


ISBN 0-938655-45-0

# CONTENTS

# MATTING

## PRESENTATION

Matting is a border that surrounds the artwork. Although the mat serves important practical functions, it has an aesthetic purpose as well. It can be used to highlight a color in the artwork, accent a shape, or simply increase the size to make a dramatic display (especially for small pieces). Matting may consist of a single, double or triple mat. Double and triple mats create a narrow, accent strip of matting which enhances the item to be framed.

## SUPPORT

The mat and its backing board provide support for artwork by allowing hinges or other means of attachment to be hidden from view. Artwork may be attached to the underside of the window mat if the picture is small, or to the backboard for larger pieces.

## AIR CIRCULATION

A mat allows air circulation between the art and the glass or plastic glazing material. Pictures, photographs, or needlework should not be placed directly against glass because moisture that condenses inside a framed piece becomes trapped and could cause mildew, mold and buckling. Work pressed against glass may also stick to the glass.

## EXPANSION

Because paper expands and contracts with changes in humidity in the environment, space must be allowed within a frame for the paper to "move" from side to side and top to bottom. Artwork properly suspended in a mat has room for these movements. If a mat is not used, other support, such as full mounting, will be required, and perhaps a spacer in the frame to provide important "breathing space" between artwork and glass.

# SELECTING A COLOR

To design perfect framing, make a selection by considering one of the three most often used criteria:

    A. The art — a decision based solely on the merits of the artwork, its colors, textures and subject matter.

    B. The background — how the artwork will coordinate with its intended surroundings.

    C. Personal preferences — such as favorite colors.

### THE ART

The work being framed could be anything: a watercolor, a limited edition print, a poster, baseball cards, lead soldiers, a plate, a certificate, a pair of gloves or coins. When the item was created, the colors and shapes were selected to convey a design.

Look at the piece carefully and note the colors that are most prominent: which color covers the most area and which the least? Select the colors to match and use them in the same proportions. For example, when framing a watercolor, the largest portion of color may be represented by the paper or the actual paint on the paper. If a great deal of white watercolor paper is visible, a white mat with a liner mat of one of the more prominent colors would be appropriate. If the painting is fully covered with paint, a color for the mat should be selected from the most prominent paint colors.

When searching for the overall design, look for the artist's or designer's intent. Consider the size, the texture, and the lines of the piece. Is there an overall "feeling" that should be considered while selecting the presentation? Are the colors opaque, transparent, bold, pale, bright, thick, or thin? Overall, is the piece bold, strong, heavy, light, airy, delicate, fine, watery, contemporary or antique? Select a matting board that will echo these same qualities. There are hundreds of matboards available in all types of colors and finishes. The main mat color can be selected from the most prominent color while the liner mat can be an accent color.

Strive to duplicate the colors and "feel" of the piece in the framing. The art and framing should be compatible — a balanced composition.

## THE BACKGROUND

Where will the piece hang? Is the wall light, medium, or dark? Is it painted, patterned, or textured? When working with a patterned wall, the art will need a wide mat to keep it from being lost.

Should the room design be reflected in the presentation? Should the framing package match the wall color? Often decorators select mat colors to match wall colorings. This is practically impossible due to the different textures of matboards and walls. Picture framing glass may also cause a problem because it often has a slight tint of color that affects the match.

## PERSONAL PREFERENCE

This color choice does not have to make sense. If a mat is to be done in one's favorite color, or to match the decor of a room — great! The decision has already been made — the choices are limited to those colors. The trick will be putting those colors on the piece, then adding a representative color from the piece itself to help the art coordinate with its surroundings.

# PROPORTION

Proportion is something one sees rather than measures. It is personal visual perception of the balance of light, color, texture, shape and line direction.

When everything within the design has proper placement, size and intensity, good composition and balance of proportion has been achieved. When designing matting and framing for the artwork, harmony among all elements should be sought.

Do not underestimate the importance of good design in framing. Let the design of the artwork itself help guide the decision making.

Consider the following descriptive words that may characterize the artwork being framed. They can also help determine the type of framing that will be suitable.

- Is the coloring light, dark, intense, dull, pale, washed or roughly applied?
- Are the lines in the artwork delicate, broad, busy, or strong?
- Are the shapes round, square, small, large, mixed, open or solid?
- Is the texture smooth, rough, intricate, bold or multi-layered?
- Is the mood somber, fanciful, powerful, or restrained?

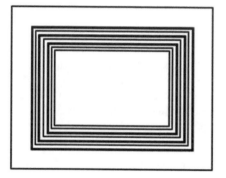

The decorative lines are overpowering and would be more prominent than the artwork.

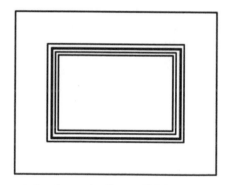

A few decorative lines will bring attention to the artwork by highlighting colors and therefore drawing the eye into the art.

When deciding how wide the matboards should be, creating a pleasing appearance is the only rule. However, there are some helpful general hints:

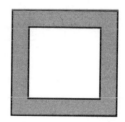

- Do not be afraid of large mat borders. They can create a visually pleasing "breathing space" between the artwork and the frame.

- Small, narrow mats tend to distract the eye with too many patterns of lines surrounding the artwork.

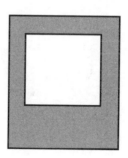

- The width of the mat and mouldings should be decidedly different. If the matting is 2" wide, the moulding should be at least 3" wide or 1" wide.

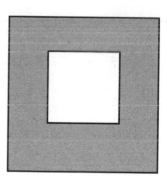

Note the effect of using the same size openings within various outside dimensions.

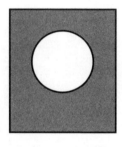 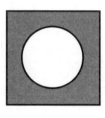 

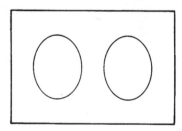

The border and center width are the same. This causes the ovals to separate.

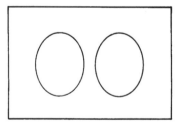

By reducing the center space between the ovals the artwork is centered. This look provides good balance while featuring the artwork.

# MAT STYLES

A popular mat style uses equal margins on all four sides.  Part of the reason for the popularity of this even-on-all-sides mat is the ease and speed of cutting them with straight-line mat cutters.   Even-border mats are attractive and they provide that important sense of balance for many artwork pieces.

Another style of mat, often considered traditional,  is weighted at the bottom with an extra width of matting.   Some people feel strongly about which of the two styles they prefer; others make their selection based on the best presentation for each piece.

The choice of even borders or a weighted bottom should be made on the basis of good design and composition which would include all elements of the framing: the artwork, the mat, and the frame.

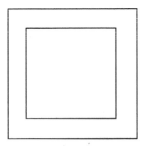

Even-on-all-sides mat

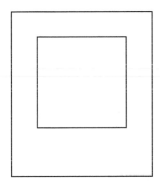

This has extra width at the
bottom border.

# Standard Sizes

It is important to know the standard sizes for the art and framing industry, since mats and boards are often made to standard sizes, glass is often pre-cut to these sizes and many ready-made frames are available in them.

Knowing these sizes will help in choosing the proper size for artwork with regard to availability of framing materials.  It is far easier to use a lite of precut 16 x 20" glass than to trim a lite of glass to 15 x 19-7/8".

Remember the limitations. All matboards are available in 32 x 40".   Some of the more popular colors are available in 40 x 60" and a few boards, such as rag matboard, are made to 4 x 8'.  Check with the suppliers.

The following is a list of the standard sizes found in the art, craft and picture framing industry:

| | | |
|---|---|---|
| 4x5 | **11x14** | **24x36** |
| 4x6 | 12x16 | 26x32 |
| **5x7** | 14x18 | **30x40** |
| 6x8 | **16x20** | 32x40 |
| **8x10** | 18x24 | 36x48 |
| 8x12 | **20x24** ✓ | 40x60 |
| 8-1/2x11 | 22x28 | 48x60 |
| 9x12 | **24x30** | 48x96 |

*Although ready-made frames and mats are available in many sizes, the sizes printed in bold are the most common.*

20x24 special order at Wallock's

# DESIGNING WITH STANDARD SIZES

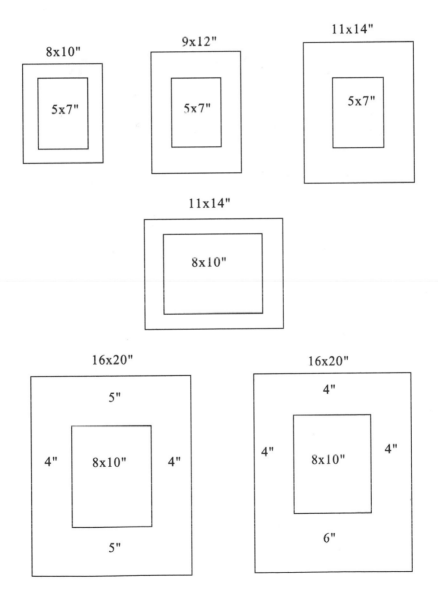

8x10"

5x7"

9x12"

5x7"

11x14"

5x7"

11x14"

8x10"

16x20"

5"

4"    8x10"    4"

5"

16x20"

4"

4"    8x10"    4"

6"

16x20"

11x14"

20x24"

11x14"

20x24"

10 x 10"

16x20"

8x8"

# MEASURING FOR MATS

Measuring should be done with a quality wooden carpenter's rule or artist's rule. An ⅛" difference could result in buckled artwork, so do not take chances with the ruler. Cloth measuring tapes and yardsticks are not accurate. For framing purposes, frames are measured from the back side of the frame along the inside edge, or rabbet. This measurement is required because the rabbet accommodates the mats and glass.

Lay the frame face down and use a ruler inside the rabbet to determine the size from end to end for both the width and the height. The rabbet size of ready-made and custom frames should be slightly larger than the mat, glass and backing. A so-called 8 x 10" frame should actually measure 8⅛ x 10⅛" when measured tightly from end to end, inside the rabbet. This allows a comfortable fit for the other materials, and leaves a bit of space for expansion of mat and backing boards as they react to changes in heat and humidity.

Remember to provide the fractional allowance when cutting or ordering materials to fit a frame. The materials must be fractionally smaller than the tight end-to-end measurement of the frame. For example, the frame measured from end-to-end is actually 8⅛x 10⅛", but the outside dimensions of the mat measures exactly 8 x 10".

To figure the dimensions of a mat, determine the size of the opening (window) by measuring the artwork to be matted. The mat must overlap each edge of the artwork by at least 1/8" in order to prevent those edges from peeking through or actually lifting out into the mat opening.

After the proper opening is established, add the amount of matting desired.

1. Add the amount of both side borders to the horizontal opening measurement.
2. Add the width of both the top and bottom borders to the vertical opening measurement.

It is often necessary to add the extra fractions to the border size so that the measurements become round numbers which are easier to work with. For example:

An 8 x 12" photograph has an actual opening of 7¾ x 11¾". With a 3" mat border on all four sides, the outside mat edge will be 13¾ x 17¾".

By adding an ⅛" on each border (3⅛"), the result is a 14 x 18" mat—a standard size—which will also be the size of the frame and glass.

This will be true for almost every mat that is cut. Consequently, when it is stated that the dimensions of a mat opening are 8 x 10", they are probably 7¾ x 9¾", if not 7½ x 9-1/2". Always check where the mat opening will be positioned on the artwork.

Here are several examples.

13x16"

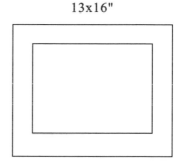

Example ONE

| 9 | x | 12" | this represents opening |
|---|---|-----|-------------------------|
| + 4 | | 4" | this represents a 2" border each side |
| 13 | x | 16" | this is your OUTSIDE mat size |

12x16"

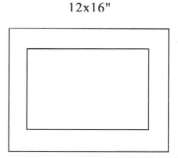

Example TWO
If the frame has already been selected, begin with the frame size and subtract the desired mat opening to determine border size.

| 12 | x | 16" | frame size |
|----|---|-----|------------|
| - 8 | x | 12" | opening size |
| 4 | x | 4" | 2" border each side |

Example THREE
When matting will not be equal on all sides, either because the artwork does not fit the chosen frame evenly, or because different proportions are preferred for the mat, divide the available border equally, or use extra at the bottom.

| 11 | x | 14" | frame size |
|----|---|-----|------------|
| - 8 | x | 10" | opening size |
| 3 | x | 4" | difference to be divided between the borders |

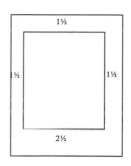

Make the mat border either:
  1½" sides, 2" top and bottom
  or 1½" top and sides, 2½" bottom.

Many mat sizes will not allow the convenience of working with whole inches. Become familiar with adding, subtracting, and dividing fractions. For example:

Example FOUR
An old frame measures 14½ x 21¾". The best mat opening for the vertical picture that will be placed in the frame is 8¾ x 15".

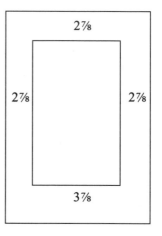

| | | |
|---|---|---|
| 14½ | x  21¾" | frame size |
| - 8¾ | x  15" | mat opening |
| 5¾ | 6¾" | available border |

It is decided that the mat border will be the same on top and at the sides, with extra at the bottom. Divide the 5¾" in half to determine the side border. It will be 2⅞" on each side. Since this will also be the top border amount, subtract 2⅞" from the 6¾" available. This leaves 3⅞", which will be the lower mat border.

Example FIVE
Two 5 x 7" photos in one mat.

openings — 4½ x 6½"
top and bottom — 2¼"
sides — 2"
center space — 1"

Add the:

| horizontal measurements | vertical measurements |
|---|---|
| 2 | |
| 4½ | |
| 1 | 2¼ |
| 4½ | 6½ |
| + 2 | + 2¼ |
| 14 | 11 |

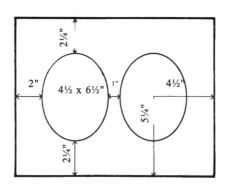

Example SIX
Double matted 8 x 12" photo.
Frame size 16 x 20".

    opening — 7½ x 11½"
    borders — 4"
    liner — 3"


    16    x    20"    frame size
 -  7½  x    11½"  opening
    8½   x    8½

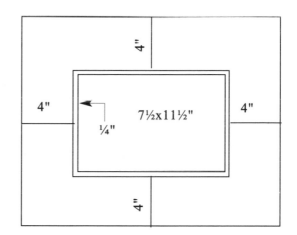

Example SEVEN
Single matted 8 x 12" photo.
Frame size 14 x 18".


    14    x    18"    frame size
 -  7½  x    11½"  opening
      6½        6½"

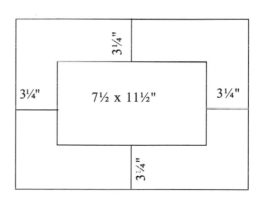

# TRIMMING A MATBOARD TO SIZE

Most matboards are available in the standard
32 x 40" size. The actual size of the board
will be a fraction larger to allow for changes
in humidity during shipping and storage.
A perfectly square matboard is possible by
trimming off the excess.

Depending upon the style of cutter, the
matboards may have to be cut before they can
be used. Check the instructions that come
with the cutter — they should state the
maximum size board the machine will
accommodate.

It is imperative the matboard be trimmed
exactly square — take extra care to cut it
correctly and keep the cutter square. The
owner's manual will have directions on
squaring the cutter.

Use the best equipment available — the better
the equipment, the better the results. Mat
cutting is a precision craft. Good tools and
measurements are a necessity.

# TRIMMING A BOARD USING THE HAND-HELD CUTTER AND A T-SQUARE

Trimming matboards to size requires a straightedge or T-square, a hand-held cutter and a sturdy, flat worktable.

Lay the matboard *face down* on the table and measure off the sizes required using a pencil and an accurate rule.

To trim the board down to size:

1. Lay a scrap of matboard on the table surface and set the measured-off mat board *face down* on top of the scrap board.

2. Set the T-square in place on the penciled line.

3. Set the cutting head on the edge of the rule, insert the blade into the board and pull the cutter. Be careful as the cutter comes close to the edge of the table. If a board is very thick, a couple of passes on the same cut may be taken to get through the board; it is not necessary to cut through a board in one swipe.

4. Check each piece for squareness. Making a perfect mat begins with a perfect board.

Use the straight cutter to trim matboards.

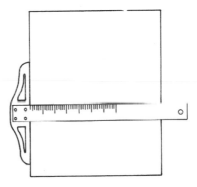

# TRIMMING A BOARD USING THE
## *COMPACT* MAT CUTTER

1. Use a ruler and pencil to measure off the size board required. The board must be less than 30" to fit in the *Compact* mat cutter. If the board is larger, use the directions on page 21 to reduce the size before continuing with the following instructions.

2. Remove the side mat guide.

3. Measure the size board needed. Pencil mark the cutting places.

4. Insert the matboard into the cutter *face down*.

5. Using the 90-degree straight cutter, slice the board to the desired size.

Use the straight cutter to trim matboards.

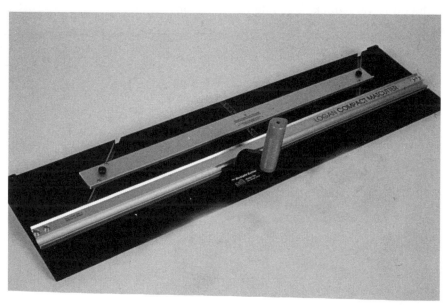

# TRIMMING A BOARD USING THE
# *SIMPLEX PLUS* MAT CUTTER

1. Place the cutter a on flat, fully supported, solid surface. Affix the squaring arm, if the cutter is equipped with one.

2. Insert the matboard at the lower right. Position the board to the exact measurement for the outside dimension.

Use the straight cutter to trim matboards.

3. Slip the straight-cutter onto the guide rail at the top of the board and pull all the way from the top of the board to the bottom.

The depth of the blade may be adjusted to cut through regular matboard or thicker foam center board.

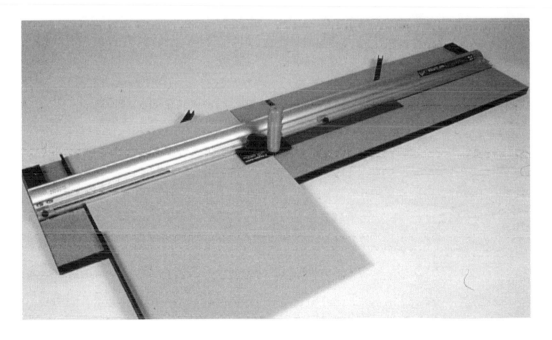

# MAKING THE MOST
# OF A 32x40" MATBOARD

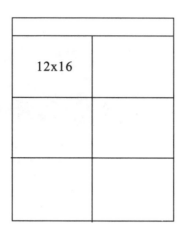

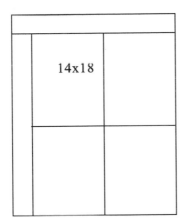

14x18

8x10

16x20

8x10

18x24

24x36

8x10

9x12

18x24

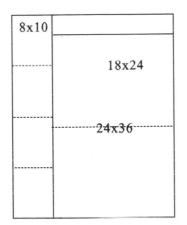

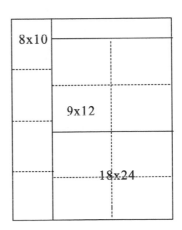

# MAT CUTTING

Mat cutting is an art. A well-done, custom-made mat is the result of quality materials, a quality mat cutter and practice.

To get a mat cutter in tip-top condition, look over the owner's manual that came with the cutter. The time will be well-spent and will save wasted materials and wracked nerves.

CHECK LIST

____ The base of the mat cutter must be fully supported and level.

____ Use a perfect T-square when measuring. (Make sure the head does not wobble, etc.)

____ Use a slip sheet — a scrap matboard — on the face of the cutting board.

____ Check the depth of the blade. It must slice through the matboard and scratch the slip sheet.

____ Use sharp blades — always. It is cheaper to throw away pennies for a new blade than dollars for the matboard.

____ Do not jab the blade into the matboard — slide it into position.

____ Try to keep the boards in a dry place as damp boards are harder to cut than dry boards.

# CUTTING A SINGLE MAT
## USING A HAND-HELD CUTTER

1. Trim the matboard to size.

2. Using a pencil and T-square, measure and mark the back side of the matboard.

3. Place the mat *face down* on a piece of scrap matboard that is larger than the board that is to be cut.

4. Slide both boards to the closest edge of the table. Leaning against the head of the T-square will help to hold it in position while cutting the mat.

5. Set the T-square on the penciled line.

6. Set the cutter against the T-square and line up the silver guide line on the cutting head with the pencil line.

7. If mat cutter style #1100 or #2000 is being used, insert the blade and *push* the blade and handle towards the top.

   If style #4000 is being used, start at the top, insert the blade into the mat and *pull* the cutting head towards the bottom.

8. Cut all four sides in the same manner. Be careful to stop and start accurately.

Logan #1100 push style
hand-held cutter

Logan #2000 push style
hand-held cutter

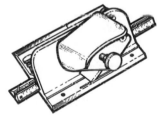

Logan #4000 pull style
hand-held cutter

# CUTTING A SINGLE MAT
## USING THE *TEAM SYSTEM*

1. Trim the matboard to size.

2. Place the matboard *face down* on a piece of scrap matboard that is larger than the board that is to be cut. This will protect the both the face of the mat and the table surface.

3. Using a pencil and the scale, measure and mark the back side of the matboard to indicate the required window opening of the mat.

4. Slide both boards to the closest edge of the table.

5. Place the guide rail directly on the left-hand border. Position the outside edge of the guide rail with the penciled line.

6. Attach the mat cutter to the guide rail by fitting the nylon guides over the raised edge of the channel. Position the silver guide line on the mat cutter even with the bottom intersecting pencil line.

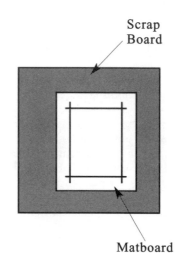

Scrap Board

Matboard

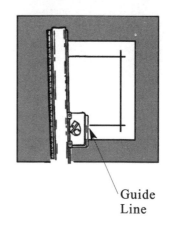

Guide Line

7. The right thumb should push down on the thumb divot until the blade is through the mat. Fingers should curl under the Sidewall of the mat cutter while the palm is behind the mat cutter.

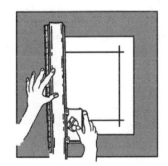

8. Push the cutting head forward towards the top with constant pressure until the silver guide line is even with the top intersecting pencil line.

9. Cut the other three sides in the same manner.

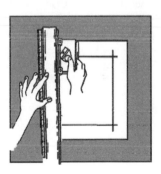

To Cut Left-handed: Place the guide rail on the right-hand border. Line up the silver indicator line with the top intersecting pencil line. Place fingertips on the thumb divot and pull downward until the silver indicator line lines up with the bottom intersecting pencil line.

# Cutting a Single Mat
## using the *Compact* Mat Cutter

These directions are for an
    11 x 14" mat
    5 x 8" opening
    with a 3" border on all sides.

1. Slide a slip sheet onto the base of the cutter. Slip sheets are made from scraps of matboard approximately 6" wide by 20" to 30". A much neater cut will be achieved by using a slip sheet.

Logan #2000 The LOGAN cutting head has silver markings on the bevel cutting head to indicate the stop and start. Align the markings with the penciled lines. No guessing required.

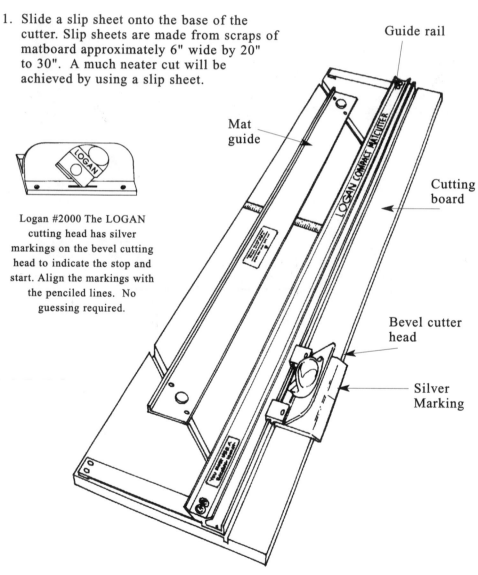

Guide rail

Mat guide

Cutting board

Bevel cutter head

Silver Marking

2. Set the side mat guide at 3". To set the mat guide: loosen the black knobs and press down on them until they click, then slide the guide into position.

3. Take the trimmed 11 x 14" matboard and slide it *face down* under the guide rail and against the side mat guide.

4. Using a pencil, draw a line against the rail onto the matboard. Repeat this on the other three sides. The lines must be long enough to intersect.

5. Set the bevel cutter at the bottom intersection where the pencil mark intersects the rail edge. Line up the silver marking on the side of the cutter with the pencil line.

6. Hold the cutting head still with the left hand while pushing the blade into the board.

7. Push the bevel cutter forward and stop on the pencil mark intersection at the top of the mat.

8. Repeat this procedure on the remaining three sides.

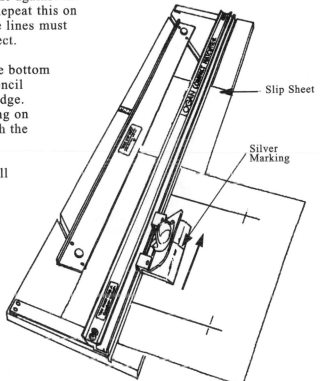

Slip Sheet

Silver
Marking

# Cutting a Single Mat
## using the *Simplex Plus* Mat Cutter

These directions are for an
    11 x 14" mat
    5 x 8" opening
    with a 3" border on all sides.

1. Set the mat guide and guide rail stop at 3".
   To set the mat guide: loosen the black
   knobs and press down on the until they
   click, then slide the guide into position.
   Set the guide rail stop at the 3" mark at the
   bottom of the cutter.

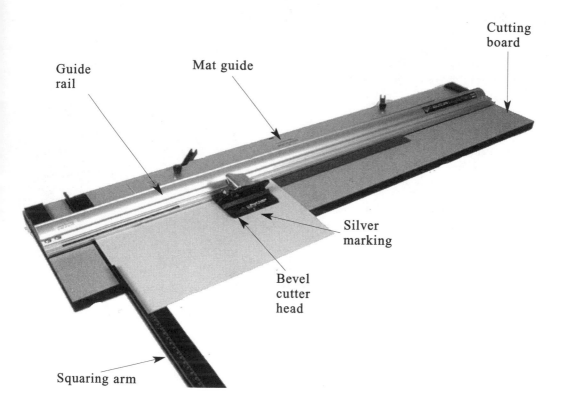

Cutting
board

Guide
rail

Mat guide

Silver
marking

Bevel
cutter
head

Squaring arm

2. Place the mat *face down* in the cutter on top of the slip sheet. Make sure the board is flush with the mat guide and squaring arm.

3. Using the edge of the guide rail, draw a line with a pencil from the top to the bottom of the matboard.

4. Lift the guide rail and rotate the mat one-quarter turn clockwise. Set the mat back in *face down*.

5. Place the bevel cutting head on the guide rail, at the top of the mat.

6. Line up the silver guide line on the cutting head with the pencil mark. Insert the blade into the board and *pull* towards the guide rail stop.

7. Lift the guide rail and rotate the mat one-quarter turn clockwise.

8. Line up the silver guide line with the cut that was just made. Insert the blade into the board and pull towards the squaring arm. Repeat this procedure on the remaining sides.

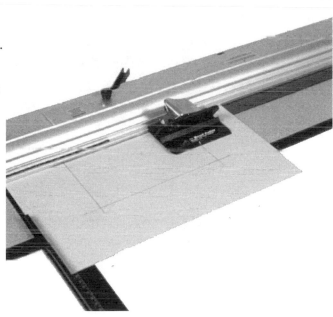

# CUTTING A DOUBLE MAT
## METHOD ONE

1. Trim two matboards 11 x 14":
    White for the top mat
    Gray for the undermat.

2. Set mat guides at 3".

3. Slide the Gray board into the cutter
   *face down*. Make sure to use a slip
   sheet.

4. Cut all four sides of the Gray mat.

5. Set mat guides at 2¾".

6. Slide in the White board into the cutter *face down*.

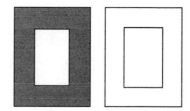

7. Cut all four borders.

8. Tape the two boards together at the top edge of the mats. Often tape is used all around the edges of the mats, however when mats are larger than 11 x 14", the tape may cause buckling. It is best to use tape on the top side to allow the boards to expand and contract with changes in humidity.

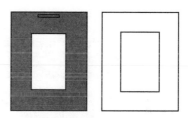

Attach the two mats together with
double-sided tape or a small
amount of white glue.

# METHOD TWO — THE PERFECT DOUBLE MAT

This method of cutting double mats will result with a perfect border every time.

1. Trim a Gray 11 x 14" top mat.
   Trim a White 10¾ x 13¾" liner.

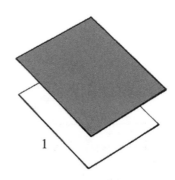

2. Set a slip sheet in the cutter. Put Gray board into cutter *face down* and cut a 2¾" border; save the fallout.

3. Apply four strips of double-sided tape on the face of the White board and attach it to the back side of the Gray board.

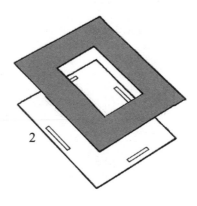

4. Take the Gray fallout and tape it back into place with a 1" strip of double-sided tape to make it easier to cut the next opening.

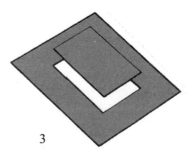

5. Set mat guides at 3".

6. Insert the two taped-together mats *face down* with the fallout in place and cut the 3" border on all four sides.

The purpose of cutting the liner matboard smaller is to keep it from interfering with the measurements on the first set of cuts.

NOTE: Remove the tape from the sides and bottom. Often tape is used all around the edges of the mats, however when mats are larger than 11 x 14", the tape may cause buckling. It is best to use tape on the top side to allow the boards to expand and contract with changes in humidity.

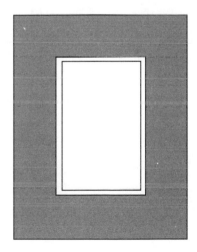

# Cutting a Double Mat
## using the Hand-held Cutter

1. Trim two matboards to exactly 11 x 14".
   Gray is the top mat.
   White is the liner mat.

2. Using a pencil and a T-square, measure
   and mark the back side of the matboards
   for the two different size borders required
   for the double mat.

3. Mark the Gray mat with a 2½" border.

4. Mark the White mat with a 3" border.

5. Place the mat *face down* on a piece of
   scrap matboard that is larger than the
   board that is to be cut.

6. Slide both boards to the closest edge of
   the table.  Leaning against the head of
   the T-square will help to hold it in
   position while cutting the mat.

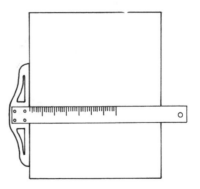

7. Set the T-square on the penciled line.

8. Set the cutter against the T-square and
   line up the silver guide line on the
   cutting head with the pencil line.

9. If mat cutter style #1100 or #2000 is being used, insert the blade and *push* the blade and handle towards the top.

If style #4000 is being used, start at the top, insert the blade into the mat and *pull* the cutting head towards the bottom.

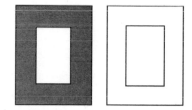

10. Cut all four sides in the same manner. Be careful to stop and start accurately.

11. Remove the fallout piece and set aside.

12. Repeat steps 5 through 9 for the second mat.

13. Tape the two boards together at the top edge of the mats. Often tape is used all around the edges of the mats, however when mats are larger than 11 x 14", the tape may cause buckling. It is best to use tape on the top side to allow the boards to expand and contract with changes in humidity.

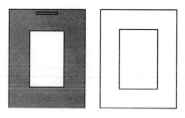

# CUTTING AN OFFSET MAT

1. Measure off back side of mat
   (as shown) — two sets of lines: one set
   3" from edge, one set 3¼" from edge.

2. Set mat guide at 3". Insert board
   *face down* and cut the two long sides,
   being careful to start and stop at the 3¼"
   top and bottom measurements.

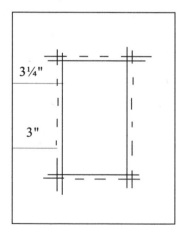

3. Cut the two short sides, stopping at the 3¼" mark. The center will not drop out.

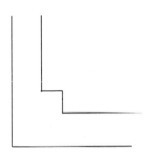

4. Reset guide at 3¼". Insert matboard *face down* and cut four more sides connecting the cuts to form the angle corner.

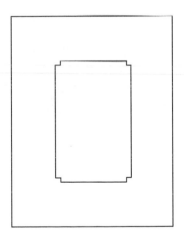

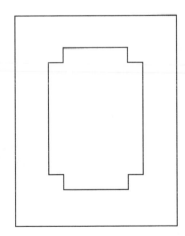

# CUTTING A V-GROOVE
## USING A MAT CUTTER

V-grooves are cut into the matboard by directing bevel cuts to face each other, creating a "V" shape.

1. Set guide rail for a 2" border.

2. Pencil off the 2" border.

3. Insert the matboard *face down* into cutter and cut three sides.

4. Before cutting the fourth side, place tape over the three cuts to keep the center from dropping out.

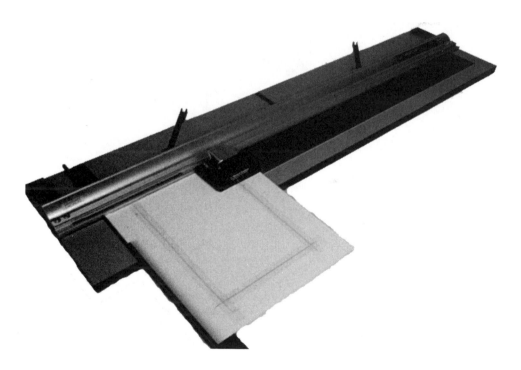

5. Cut the fourth side.

6. Lift mat out of cutter, flip over and place the board back into the cutter, *face up*.

7. Do not change the 2" border. Insert the cutting head at the intersection of the existing cut and guide the cutter along the cut. Cut all four sides.

8. The center will drop out — tape it back in and reset the guide bar for 3".

9. Place the taped board back into the cutter *face down*. Cut the mat as usual. The center will drop out. The result is a 3" border mat with a V-groove 1" from the window opening.

# Cutting a V-groove
## using the *Simplex Plus V-Groover*

1. Set squaring arm stop at 2".

2. Place spacer bars flat against stop.  If spacer bars are not being used, set the stop ½" less than the desired V-groove measurement.

3. Set the guide rail stop at 2".

4. Place matboard in cutter *face up*.

5. Place V-groove stop onto guide rail and lock into place.  Make sure the the foot of the stop rests against the top edge of the matboard.  Set scale at 2".

6. Place the thumb of right hand on the V-groove label and place the index and middle fingers on the front of the base.

7. Use left hand to push on the left lever handle (note arrow direction on lever), hold down and *push* the cutting head from the bottom to the top (the V-groove stop).

8. Use left hand to push on the right lever handle (note arrow direction on lever), hold down and *pull* the cutting head from the top to the bottom.

9. Reposition the matboard and cut the remaining three sides.

If corners are still slightly connected after all four sides have been cut, use a razor blade to carefully finish the separation.

# CUTTING AN INLAY MAT

1. Cut one board 11 x 14".

2. Cut the inlay board ¼" smaller.

3. Adhere the mats together by placing a *small amount* of double-sided tape on the face of the smaller board — towards the outside edge.

4. Set the mat guide and stops to 3". Put the layers into the cutter, *face down*, and cut a 3" border on all four sides. The inlay opening has just been cut. The boards will stay together.

5. Remove the stops and set the mat guide at 2½".

6. Return the "sandwich" *face down* into the cutter. Cut a bevel from the top edge to the bottom edge on all four sides (cutting through one board only). The corners of the smaller board will fall away. The sides will have to be pulled off because the tape is holding them in place. The inlay will slide off. Save it.

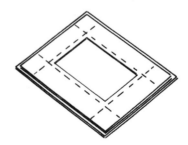

7. Place the larger mat in the cutter *face down*. Cut using the same guide setting of 2½". Set the blade to cut through one board and scratch the second board or slip sheet. Discard fallout.

8. Put the inlay into the mat opening and tape the back side.

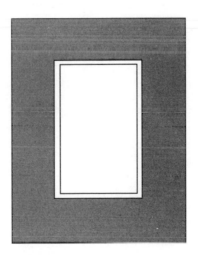

# OVAL & CIRCLE MATS

Oval and circle mats must be made with a machine that can cut a precise circle or ellipse through matboard. It is nearly impossible to cut an oval or circle with a scissors or hand-held utility knife.

Oval openings are suited to artwork that has a centralized image. Since the corners will be concealed, the oval can be used to cover unwanted corners or eliminate unnecessary space.

When planning the size border of an oval or circle it is important to consider the size space that will be left at the corners. It will be considerably larger. The space created at the corners is especially suited to added decoration.

Logan *3-Step Oval and Circle Mat Cutter* #201

# CUTTING A CIRCLE MAT

The following directions are for a 10 x 10"
mat with a 6" circle opening.

1. Trim a matboard to 10 x 10". Place the
   mat *face up* on the work surface with a
   scrap board, larger than the mat, as
   a slip sheet.

2. Adjust the cutting unit to cut a 6" circle
   by setting the scale arm to 6". Then set
   the scale inside the oval base at zero (0).

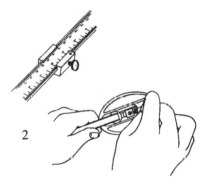

2

3. Push the stepping lever down until it
   stops. This will keep the blade from
   touching the board prematurely.

4. Draw four lines on the face of the mat to
   intersect at the precise center of the oval.

5. Place the base directly on the
   intersection, coordinating the markings
   on the base.

6. Press on the base so that the base pins
   penetrate the matboard. Make sure the
   base is flat on the board.

7. Hold down base with one hand and place
   right hand on scale arm with thumb on
   top of the adjustment block. Lift the
   stepping lever to the first of three
   positions.

5

8. Rotate the blade around by one of two methods:
   a) Pull the scale arm one quarter of the way, rotate the matboard and cut another quarter until the blade reaches its initial point of entry.

OR
   b) Hold base with left hand and pull blade one half of the way and then switch hands. Hold the base with right hand and pull blade the rest of the way.

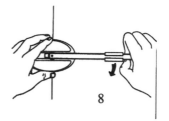

9. Lift stepping lever to the second setting and rotate around board.

10. Lift stepping lever to the third setting and make the final revolution.

11. Before removing base, make sure that the blade has cut completely through the board. If it has not, make another revolution.

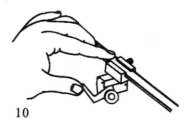

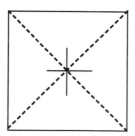

Find the center of placement for the oval or circle

# CUTTING AN OVAL

To cut an oval mat, follow the same
directions used for cutting a circle mat
except the settings will be different.

 1

For example:

To set the scales for a 5 x 7" opening:

1.  Set the scale arm to 5".

2.  Set the adjustable slide scale (inside
    the oval base) for the difference
    between the height and width of the
    oval.  7 - 5 = 2.  Therefore, set the
    adjustable slide scale at 2".

 2

3.  Continue with steps 3 through 12 on
    page 49 and 50.

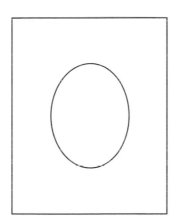

# CUTTING A
# DOUBLE OVAL

1. Trim two 11 x 14" matboards:
   White for the top mat.
   Black for the liner mat.

2. Apply double-sided tape to the face of the Black mat. Put a strip on each of the four sides of the face as near as possible to the edge of the mat.

3. Carefully align the outside edges of the White mat and the liner mat and press them together so that the back of the White mat is adhered to the face of the Black mat.

4. Draw two intersecting lines on the face of the White mat. They should intersect at right angles in the precise position where the center of the double oval is desired.

5. Set the adjustable slide scale for 2".

6. Set the scale arm for 8".

7. Position the base of the front of the mat so that the indicator notches line up with the intersecting lines. Press the base down and cut an oval. (See Cutting an Oval on page 51).

8. Remove the base to allow the fallout to drop out. The Black mat will not be cut and the indentations from the base will be present.

9. Set the scale arm for 7½".

10. Position the base in the indentations previously made and cut an oval.

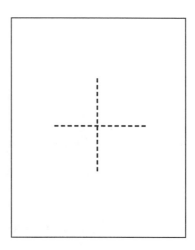

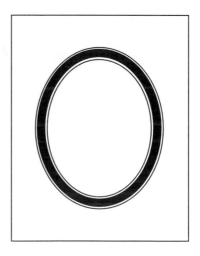

# CUTTING AN OVAL INLAY

1. Trim two pieces of 11 x 14" matboard.
   White will be the top mat.
   Black will be the inlay mat.

2. Draw two lines on the face of the White
   mat so that they intersect at right angles in
   the precise position where the center of the
   oval is desired.

3. Set the adjustable slide scale at 2".

4. Set the scale arm to 9".

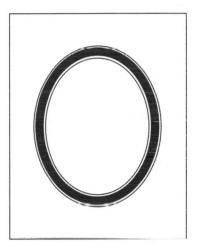

5. Position the base of the front of the White
   mat so that the indicator notches line up
   with the intersecting lines. Press the base
   down and cut an oval. (See Cutting an
   Oval). IMPORTANT: Do not make any
   adjustments to the scale arm. It is essential
   that the dimensions for the oval remain
   exactly the same for the next cut.

6. Position the base on the face of the Black
   mat. Press the base down and cut an oval.
   Keep the fallout.

7. Adjust the scale arm to 8".

8. In the fallout piece of the Black mat there
   will be four holes which were made by the
   base pins. Position the base in the holes,
   press down and cut an oval.

9. Take the resulting ring and fit it flush into
   the window opening of the White Mat.
   Tape the back.

# CUTTING A ROMAN MAT

1. Trim a matboard to 11 x 14".

2. Measure 2½" on the sides and bottom.

3. Measure 5½" from the top and find the true center of the board. This will be the starting position for the oval.

4. Cut a 5 x 7" oval (see Cutting a Circle on page 49). Tape the dropout back in place with removable tape. This supports the matboard while the remaining cuts are made.

5. Measure 4¼" from the top and cut two small slices on each side of the oval with a mat cutter.

6. Place matboard *face down* in cutter and cut the 2½" border on the sides and the bottom.

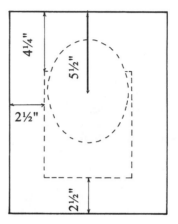

# CUTTING AN
# ARCH MAT

1. Cut a matboard 11 x 14".

2. Measure off 2½" on sides and bottom.

3. Measure in 5½" from the sides and top to find the center of the circle.

4. Cut a 6" circle (see Cutting a Circle on page 49) from that point.  Tape the dropout back in place with removable tape before proceeding.

5. Using the straight-line cutter, cut the sides and bottom.  Take care on the join of the circle and sides.  Use an emery board to smooth out rough connections.

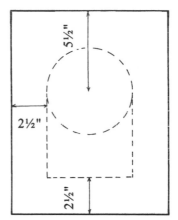

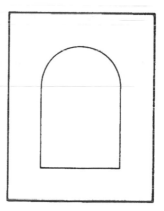

# CUTTING A SCALLOPED CIRCLE

1. Trim an 11 x 14" matboard.

2. Draw two lines on the face of the mat so that they intersect at right angles in the precise center of the mat, resulting in a cross.

3. Lay a straightedge from the bottom left corner to the top right corner of the mat and draw a line that bisects the cross at an angle. Lay the straightedge from the bottom right corner to the top left corner and draw another line that bisects the cross at an angle. The lines do not need to be more than 6" long.

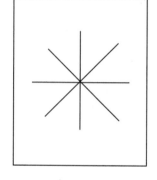

4. Select a backing sheet that is at least the same size as the mat that will be cut. Apply double-sided tape in a grid fashion to the backing sheet. Lay five strips vertically and five strips horizontally. The strips should run the full length of the backing sheet. The outer strips should be as near as possible to the outside edge of the mat.

5. Lay the mat *face up* on the backing sheet and adhere them together by pressing down.

6. Position the base of the front of the mat so that the indicator notches line up with the original intersecting lines. Press the base down and cut an oval. (See Cutting an Oval). NOTE: When the cut is finished the fallout piece will not fall free. Do not attempt to remove it.

7. Turn the mat one quarter turn. Position the base on the same cross so that the oval will bisect the first oval at a right angle. Press base down and cut an oval.

8. Position the base on one of the lines that runs in the direction of the mat's corners. It may be necessary to adjust the position of the base by eye without regard to the pencil lines. The object is to have the arc of the cut emerge in equal degrees above the points where the previous oval cuts intersect each other. This can be accomplished by holding the base in position (without penetrating the mat with the base pins) and rotating the scale arm to see where the blade will track. When the proper positioning has been achieved, press the base down and cut an oval. Do not remove the fallouts.

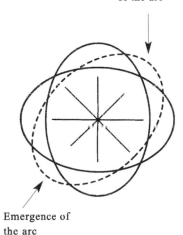

Emergence of
the arc

9. Position the base on the other line that runs in the direction of the mat's corners. Adjust the position as necessary by eye. Press the base down and cut the final oval.

10. Carefully peel the mat from the backing sheet.

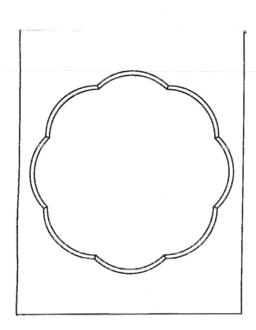

# CUTTING A VICTORIAN MAT

1. Trim an 11 x 14" matboard.

2. On the *Simplex Plus* or *Compact* mat cutter, cut a 11 x 14" mat with 2¼" borders on all four sides from the *back*.

3. Replace the fallout and tape along the cuts on the back.

4. Using the oval cutter, draw two lines on the face of the mat so that they intersect at right angles in the precise position where the center of the oval is desired.

5. Set the adjustable slide scale to 3".

6. Set the scale arm to 8".

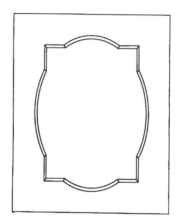

7. Position the base of the front of the mat so that the indicator notches line up with the intersecting lines. Press the base down and cut an oval. (See Cutting an Oval on page 51).

8. After the fallout piece falls free, remove the remaining tape from the back of the mat.

# MULTIPLE OPENING MATS

These types of mats are very popular for photographs and memorabilia, which means they are often several different sizes. Layout time may be more than actual cutting time. Once any plan has been worked up — save it! It may be needed again.

THE FAMILY
GROUPING

| | |
|---|---|
| outside 16 x 20" | four 3 x 3" |
| two 2 x 3" | one 3 x 4" |
| two 4 x 6" | one Overlay Name Plaque 1 x 4" |

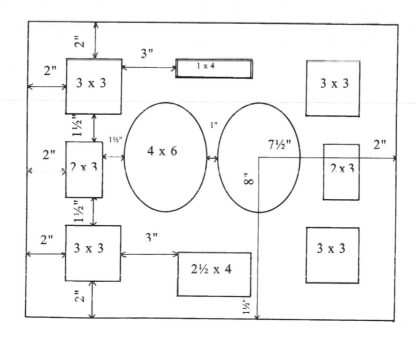

**FOUR 35mm PHOTOS**
outside 11 x 14"
four 3 x 4½"

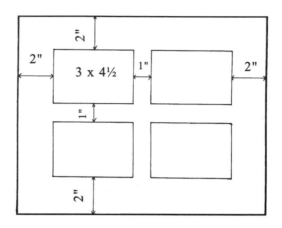

**THE ANNIVERSARY MAT**

outside 16 x 20"          three 2 x 3"
one 4½ x 6½"              four 1½ x 2"
four 3 x 4½"

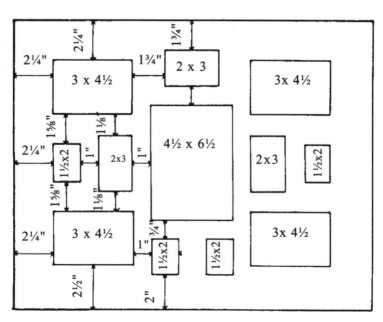

**A COUPLE**
outside 11 x 14"
two 5 x 7"

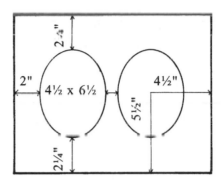

**THREE OVALS**
outside 7 x 14"
three 3 x 4"

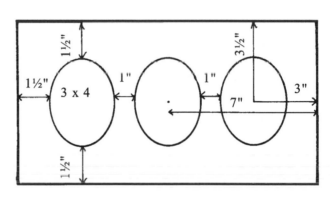

**FIVE OVALS**
outside 11 x 14"
five 3 x 3½"

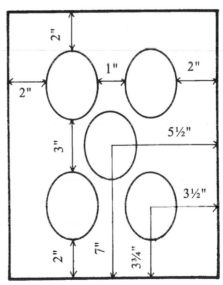

# DECORATING MATS
## USING MARBLED PAPERS

Materials:
Ruler and Pencil
Sheet of Marbled Paper
X-Acto® Knife
45° angle

Handmade marbled paper, thin wallpaper, or quality wrapping paper can be used to make narrow panels on mats.

1.  Apply a double-sided adhesive to the back side of the marbled paper.

2.  Using a hard pencil and ruler — mark areas where the paper panels are to be placed.

3.  Place the paper in the straight-line mat cutter *face up*.  Use the right-hand side of the bar as a guide.  Use an X-Acto knife to slice the small panels or lines.

4.  Place a piece of release paper in each of the four corners to keep the panels from adhering before for final placement.

5.  Peel the backing off one of the strips and carefully place it on the marked area.  Let the tape rest on the release paper in the corner.  Set the remaining strips in place.

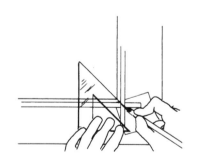

6.  Carefully pull the release paper out towards the corners.  Slice through both pieces at the  intersection.  Small tapes may be cut at a 45° angle without the aid of a ruler, but the wider tapes will require a guide to get a perfect angle.  A triangle or ruler can be used as a guide.  Slice through both strips in one stroke.  The release paper will keep the tapes from sticking to the mat.

# PRODUCT LIST
## Logan Mat Cutters

Model#        Description

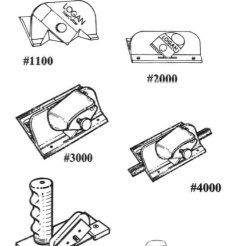

**#1100**

**#2000**

### Hand-Held Mat Cutters

1100   **Basic** Push Style mat cutter with fixed blade.

2000   **Advanced** Push style mat cutter with retractable blade.

3000   **Pro-Am** Pivot & Pull style mat cutter with pivoting blade.

4000   **Original** Pivot & Pull style mat cutter with pivoting blade and marker bar.

701    **Straight Cutter** with three depth settings. Adapts onto many Logan mat cutters.

704    **Glass Cutter** with hardened steel wheel. Adapts onto many Logan mat cutters.

1500   **Foamboard Cutter** cuts 45 & 90 degrees. Can be used against any suitable straightedge.

**#3000**

**#4000**

**#701**

**#704**

**#1500**

### Team Systems

424    **Team System** 24" ruled aluminum guide rail with 2000 mat cutter.

440    **Team System** 40" ruled aluminum guide rail with 3000 mat cutter.

441    **Team System** 40" ruled aluminum guide rail with 4000 mat cutter.

**#424**

### Board Mounted Mat Cutters

250    **Craft & Hobby Cutter** 24" base board with guide rail, squaring bars and model 500 mat knife.

301    **Compact** 32" base board with guide rail, mat guide and bevel cutting head.

301-S  **Compact** 32" base board with guide rail, mat guide, bevel cutting head and straight cutting head.

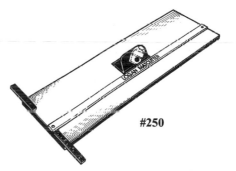

**#250**

### Instruction Books

238    Basic Mat Cutting

240    Basic Mat Decoration

242    Do It Yourself Picture Framing

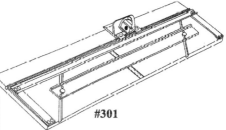

**#301**

# Logan Mat Cutters

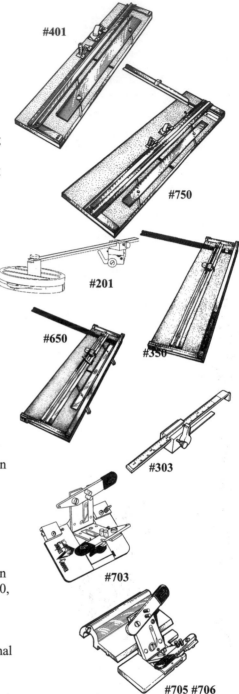

Model#      Description

401      **Intermediate** 40" base board with guide rail, mat guide, squaring bar, bevel cutting head and straight cutting head.

750      **SimplexPlus** 40" base board with guide rail, mat guide in aluminum channels, 27" squaring arm, two guide rail stops, durable laminate surface, bevel cutting head and straight cutting head.

## Oval & Circle Mat Cutter

201      **3-Step Oval & Circle** Mat Cutter includes practice matboard and 6 blades. Cuts oval from 3-1/4" x 4-3/4" to 20" x 23". Circles from 4" to 20".

## Professional Production Mat Cutters

350      **Designer's Edge** 40" base board with dual purpose straight and bevel cutting head, 27" squaring arm and production stops.

650      **Framer's Edge** 40" base board with dual purpose straight and bevel cutting head, 27" squaring arm, laminated top, mat guide and production stops.

## Surface V-Groovers

703      **Simplex V-Groover** cuts beautiful V-Grooves on the surface of the matboard. Includes stop. Operates on any #700 Simplex. Operates on #301 Compact or #401 Intermediate with the use of the **#303 Compact V-Groove Adapter.**

705      **Logan V-Groover** cuts beautiful V-Grooves on the surface of the matboard. Includes stop. Operates on any Logan Professional Production Mat Cutter including models: #310, #350, #600, #650 & #660.

706      **Logan Universal V-Groover** cuts beautiful V-Grooves on the surface of the matboard. Includes two stops. Operates on any professional mat cutter with a 5/8" thick rod on the cutting bar.

**Logan Graphic Products, Inc.**
**1100 Brown Street Wauconda, IL 60084**
**847-526-5515 Toll Free 1-800-331-6232**

*See us at* **http://www.logangraphic.com**
**E-MAIL** cs@logangraphic.com